My world, the real world and a little dose of wit!

Rachel O'Brien

BookLeaf
Publishing

My world, the real world and a little dose of wit! © 2022 Rachel O'Brien

All rights reserved.

No part of this publication may be reproduced, stored in a retrieval system, or transmitted, in any form or by any means, electronic, mechanical, photocopying, recording or otherwise, without the prior written permission of the presenters.

Rachel O'Brien asserts the moral right to be identified as author of this work.

Presentation by *BookLeaf Publishing*

Web: www.bookleafpub.com

E-mail: info@bookleafpub.com

ISBN: 9789357616720

First edition 2022

This is for my husband Ian, my daughter Lexi, my Mum Lynne and my late Dad Gareth, for hopefully being my biggest supporters.

Also to all my family, friends and loved ones lost - you are all part of who I am today. So thank you all!

I pray for you

I close my eyes and dare to dream
Of a future brighter than the sun,
A miracle, if only I can keep you safe,
An anxious wait to become your mum.

Every kick, every flutter, my heart starts to soar,
Torn between excitement and dread,
A miracle, if only I can keep you safe,
Wishes in my heart, not yet said.

My tummy grows, the stretch marks deepen,
My prayer for you, so near,
A miracle, if only I can keep you safe,
Not long until you are due to be here.

I close my eyes and dare to dream
Of a jelly bean we are yet to meet,
A miracle, if only I can keep you safe,
You will make our world complete.

A suns' descent

The sunset paints a warm
symphony of colour
onto a cool evening sky.
The golden disc sinking
down, down towards a
bashful and blushing sea.
Watch as your worries
fade away as the
sky becomes a crimson blaze.
A miracle sight as the sun
bleeds into a molten lava,
melting into the waiting water
until it finally succumbs to the moon.

Mistake

Misjudgement, or an error
Is not as bad as it may
Seem. Take a breath and
Try again. Another
Attempt could be all it needs. Be
Kind to yourself and you will
Eventually succeed!

Mirror! Mirror!

Mirror mirror on my door,
I don't like you anymore!
The reflection shows a twisted view,
Surely this image can't be true?

The light enhances the grey of my hair,
Why oh why can't you play fair?
I used to think you were so wise,
But now tree trunks have replaced my thighs.

A barrel that once was an hourglass frame,
Stares back at me with such disdain,
And let's not get started on all those chins,
Surely that's where my neck begins?

Lines now etched into once soft skin,
Maybe this is actually my evil twin?
I really don't like you anymore, so
Mirror, I'm taking you off my door!

Poor Bret

There was a young man called Bret
Who had a new mouse for a pet,
It crawled up his nose,
Slid down to his toes,
So he had to go visit the vet!

Goodbye to Primary

It started around the September,
The panic that this was the last,
The obligatory photo against the front door,
To compare with those from years before.

So much already to look forward to,
And even more to dread,
But off she goes, her head held high,
"Where's my baby gone?" I cry.

Year 6 is the year of SATS and tests,
But she does always give it her very best,
And scores don't measure who you really are,
Be confident and focussed and you will go far.

Team captain this year and a school camp away,
And she shares it all with the greatest of friends.
Growing up fast and finding her way,
I grieve for the days of stay and play.

Now primary school has come to an end,
But memories she will forever treasure,
The school will always have a place in our
hearts,
But now to move on, for a fresh new start.

My love is you

On meeting, I never dreamt that you were the
one,
But we moulded to make the perfect pair,
Together as one, through good times and bad,
You've made my dream come true,
My love is you.

Not only my love, also my best friend,
We trust each other with our lives,
Together we share our dreams and our sorrow,
I'm so grateful you love me as you do,
My love is you.

Our wedding day was my childhood dream,
One of the greatest days of my life,
A fairytale in the city of lights,
Mr and Mrs - a chapter so new,
My love is you.

We both have suffered trauma and grief,
But together we conquered and found a light,
Times have been tough, but we have each other,
Thank you for showing me a different view,
My love is you.

We now have a family, my world is complete,
You are the best husband and dad,
The memories we make and the fun we have,
A future to look forward to,
My love is you.

Life is definitely a crazy ride,
And time has proven to be a gift,
Side by side we will seize the day,
Our wish list, we will work our way through,
My love is always you!

Fireworks

Fast, flaming rockets zoom
Into the inky blanket above.
Radiant colours and whizzing worms
Exploding excitedly over the
Watching world below.
Ostentatious performance blasting it's
Rebellious bangs and crackles into a
Kaleidoscope of colour, crescendoing
into a
Spectacular and flamboyant finale.

Then it's over!

Dear Mum

Dear Mum,

Without your love, where would I be?
Every step you have been there for me,
Always willing to put your life on hold,
You really do have a heart of gold.

You sacrificed so much for me to succeed,
And your support was always guaranteed,
Even in your grief, you put me ahead,
When you were clinging on by just a thread.

My childhood was filled with laughter and fun,
And millions of memories, second to none,
Safe and loved, I could want for no more,
How lucky I feel I can't ignore.

Now as adults we enjoy quality time,
Sorting the world with a bottle of wine,
I hope you know how much you mean,
An unbreakable bond, we are a powerful team.

If I could even be a fraction of the woman you
are,
I know I could set a pretty high bar,

As a Mum and Nan, you are the best,
We really are truly blessed.

How grateful we are, I hope you know,
And also how we love you so,
Thank you for always being there for me,
Without your love, where would I be?

Is it worth it?

I huff and puff and puff and huff,
I chunner and I moan,
We are only at the first incline,
I really should get into the zone.

I puff and pant and pant and puff,
Is this torture really worth it?
A staircase up a massive hill,
Surely this will get me fit?

I groan and grumble, grumble and groan,
At least we are over half way,
Each agonising step is one step more,
It will all be worth it, they say.

I sweat and swear, swear and sweat,
Surely we are nearly there,
My thighs are screaming "how much more?"
And my lungs can't find enough air.

I breathe and gaze, gaze and breathe,
We finally reach the peak,
Breathtaking beauty, a stunning sight.
"Definitely worth it," I softly speak.

Wonders of a waterfall

A tremendous torrent cascading
Over the rock ledge.
A thunderous applause as it crashes
with such power into the plunge pool below.
An awesome, natural beauty but beneath the
surface is a formidable current, pulling deep into
the abyss unknown.
The misty spray from the collision sends an icy
blast to its enchanting surroundings, causing an
earthy, fresh scent of of the elements that alerts
the awaiting senses.
The violent rapids gush wildly downstream,
rushing recklessly and furiously until it
gradually calms and slows to a steady,gentle
flow, just tickling the pebbles as it laps elegantly
to its tranquil descent, seeping into the expectant
earth.

My Dad

With a presence that brightened any room,
And a bellowing laugh, infectious to all,
Your twinkling eyes and natural charm,
Wherever you are, you'll be having a ball.

A typical Virgo, perfection is key,
But you were always gentle and kind.
A hero whose heart was worn on his sleeve,
Such courage and strength in body and mind.

A lover of rugby, especially Wales,
You always had something to say.
How was your blood pressure always so low
After an eventful rugby day?

You worked so hard on your beautiful garden,
And your little bird guests, they loved it too,
There was nowhere else I'd rather be,
Than at your famous family barbecue.

I'm so lucky to have had such an amazing Dad,
On whom I could always depend,
A family man, so funny and loving,
The best Dad, husband and friend.

Now when I need you I look to the stars,
Or listen for your laugh in the air,
I imagine the party you are having in the skies,
And I feel comfort knowing you are there.

The monster called cancer!

You are sick, twisted, evil and cruel,
You have no mercy when you snatch a life,
You are nasty, vile, wicked and foul,
Not a care if they are a son, daughter, husband or
wife.

You are a viscous bully, scared to be seen,
You attack with demonic intent,
You are a thief who steals so many lives,
Invading, poisoning, without consent.

A sinister force, sent from below,
You are a ruthless, malevolent beast,
You are a venomous monster rotten to the core,
And on innocent bodies you choose to feast.

But you can't win, you won't succeed,
We will stand and fight to empower.
We have bonds that can't be broken,
Strength of love is our superpower!

Forever fat?

I wish I didn't like those naughty little treats,
Or indulge in those glasses of wine.
Constantly trying to stick to a diet,
But rebellion wins every time.

I wish I had more willpower,
So I didn't give in to cake,
I really wish I could be slim,
But I keep on making the same mistake.

I wish I remembered the way I feel
Every time I'm tempted by snacks,
But I always succumb to indulgence,
Then smile to cover the cracks.

I wish that I could be stronger,
So I can be proud of me,
Who knows, maybe one day,
I guess we'll just have to wait and see.

Life of a tortoise

Stomp, stomp, stomp our tortoise moves,
Straight towards his bowl of food,
Dandelions and all things green,
But what he eats is dependent on his mood.

He charges around the garden on a sunny day,
He's much faster than you'd think,
Like a dinosaur clomping, on the prowl,
Make sure you are watching, don't even blink.

He loves to soak in a cozy warm bath,
And releases bottom burps that really do smell,
Very nosy and sometimes a grump,
Any sudden movement - he shoots back in his
shell.

All he requires is heat, light and food,
And his grass and leaves are free,
But notice, I assume that he is a boy,
When in reality he could still be a she.

Growing up so fast

You are growing up so very fast,
I wish I could just stop and pause.
I remember dreaming of your arrival,
Now we bicker over the chores.

"Go away" is what you shout,
But I know it's just a stage,
You roll your eyes and tut a little
When I see tots and say "I miss you that age".

I do miss being your number one,
Just happy to go to the swings,
But you're becoming a lovely young lady,
And I'm excited for what your future brings.

I look at you and I burst with pride,
I wish I could take it all in,
You have suffered so much heartache and loss,
But still have such strength and resilience
within.

Our bond is strong but changing,
We now enjoy different activities together,
You're growing up and chasing your dreams,
And I will support you whatever.

You are funny, polite and friendly,
You are kind and loyal and true,
I really do love you with all of my soul,
And I hope you'll always be you.

You will forever be my daughter,
But baby girl inside my heart,
I will always do my best for you,
But this is your story - you're the main part.

Payday? Whatever!

I'm tired and my brain is overflowing,
I close the door on another day,
I thrive on making a real change
And that shouldn't come down to pay.

I don't have another hole in my belt,
We are supposed to work to live,
How much more can we scrimp and save?
There is nothing left to give.

We stay positive - "let's do this, it's free",
So we venture on a lovely long stroll,
But sometimes we need more to look forward to,
And the weather is sadly beyond our control.

Payday comes, I'm none the wiser,
Before I see it, it's smoke.
I really could do with a lucky win,
Or I'm going to be forever broke.

Silly Billy

There once was a lad called Billy,
Who always felt a bit chilly,
He wore big fluffy socks,
But his shoes were pink crocs,
So he thought he looked a bit silly.

My green, green soul

Green is the grass that holds my heart,
On the mountains and in the valleys,
Green is the colour of an emerald sea,
The colour that means the most to me.

Green is my favourite fruit pastille,
It is a symbol of freshness and hope,
Green is the spring that welcomes the new,
The colour of a country view.

Green is a rare four leaf clover,
The dream of finding good luck,
Green is a refreshing taste of mint,
And sometimes the colour of an envious glint.

Green is a tranquil forest,
And feeling an affinity with nature,
Green are my eyes; the window to my soul,
The colour that makes me feel whole.

Paw prints on my heart

That cold, January day we brought you home,
A timid, fearful soul,
Those chocolate eyes staring up at us,
You instantly helped to heal that hole.

You soon settled in and became our boy,
And we fell in love with your goofy smile,
Your manic leap when we got out your lead,
We could never tire you, you'd go for miles.

Snuggled on the sofa, I'd stroke your velvet ears,
You'd be nestled in the crook of my leg,
I'd rub your belly or tickle your feet,
But the first sign of food and you'd jump up to
beg.

The best big brother to our little girl,
You were the best of friends,
Together you shared joy in chasing the bubbles,
And a broken heart, you could mend.

Sunday mornings were for family fun,
We'd laugh and you would woof and woo,
Always noisy and full of love,
But this is what's real and this is true.

The field became your happy place
When walks became too tough.
We kept you happy, we kept you loved,
Until we knew you'd had enough.

My heart broke the day we said goodbye,
I didn't want us to part,
But you saved us and we saved you
And you've left paw prints on my heart.

The face behind the camera

I am the face behind the camera
And, though on the photo, I am unseen,
I am capturing the memories
Of the places I have been.

Sometimes you see my reflection,
It's proof that I was there,
Or maybe I'll snap a selfie
So in the future they are aware.

"Smile", "say cheese", "just one more"
I laugh as I snap away,
"Stop, that's enough" they cry in jest,
But they will be grateful one day.

I am the face behind the camera,
I'm sure they think I'm insane.
But when the photos are all that is left,
I hope that they will ease the pain.